THE LIFE CYCLE OF THE
HEDGEHOG

Betty Brownlie

READ BY READING

Ashton Scholastic
Auckland   Sydney   New York   Toronto   London

First published 1992

Ashton Scholastic Ltd
Private Bag 1, Penrose, Auckland 5, New Zealand.

Ashton Scholastic Pty Ltd
PO Box 579, Gosford, NSW 2250, Australia.

Scholastic Inc.
730 Broadway, New York, NY 10003, USA.

Scholastic Canada Ltd
123 Newkirk Road, Richmond Hill, Ontario L4C 3G5, Canada.

Scholastic Publications Ltd
Marlborough House, Holly Walk, Leamington Spa, Warwickshire CV32 4LS, England.

National Library of New Zealand
Cataloguing-in-Publication data

Brownlie, Betty.
  The life cycle of the hedgehog / by Betty Brownlie. Auckland, N.Z.
Ashton Scholastic, 1992.
  1 v. (Read by reading)
  ISBN 1-86943-060-3
  1. Readers–Hedgehogs. I. Title. II. Title: Hedgehog. III. Series.
Read by reading series
  428.6 (599.33)

8 7 6 5 4 3 2 1   2 3 4 5 6 7 8 9/9

Typeset by Rennies Illustrations.
Printed in Hong Kong

CONTENTS

INTRODUCTION

The hedgehog is a very common animal, found in most countries of the world.

The hedgehog is nocturnal, meaning it is active at night and sleeps during the day. It is a solitary creature, preferring to live alone. It is also a mammal, which means that the females suckle their young.

Hedgehogs can live for about ten years, but few ever reach old age. Every year millions are killed in road accidents.

WHAT HEDGEHOGS LOOK LIKE

Hedgehogs are small, plump animals with lots of prickly spines. The soft underside of the hedgehog and its face are covered in brown or very light-coloured hair. The hedgehog's very short tail is covered with only a few hairs. Male and female hedgehogs look the same.

Legs and Feet

Because the hedgehog's legs are almost hidden underneath its plump round body, they look very short. In fact, they are quite long. This means that a hedgehog can run very fast, and can easily scratch most parts of its body.

The hedgehog's feet have leathery pads underneath. Each foot has five toes with long claws. The claws on the back feet are used for grooming. The claws on the front are used for digging.

This drawing shows (a) long legs which easily scratch an itchy spot on the body, and which can run very fast, and (b) claws for grooming (hind feet), and claws for digging (front feet).

Spines

Spines protect the hedgehog against many predators such as stoats and weasels.

The spines also act as a cushion around the hedgehog's body. If the hedgehog falls from a great height, it will likely not be hurt.

The bulbous end of the spine is very strong. It will not pull out of the hedgehog's skin, even if the hedgehog is lifted up and held by only one spine. The bulbous end also prevents the spine being pushed into the hedgehog's body if the animal falls and lands heavily.

Each spine lasts for about two years and then falls out. The spines fall out one at a time, and are quickly replaced by new ones.

Drawing of spines showing actual size. Full
grown spines are about 2.5 centimetres long.
The skin beneath the spines is very thick. This
leathery skin is not easily irritated by body pests.

The sharp pointed tip of the spine provides
prickly protection against predators.

The spine is made of vertical tubes.
These tubes allow the spine to bend
without becoming permanently creased.

Curved neck of spine helps
to absorb the shock of a fall.

Bulbous end of spine
under the hedgehog's skin.

Head

The hedgehog is unable to see colours, but it has reasonable sight. Its eyes are brown to almost black in colour.

When looking for food, the hedgehog pushes its pointed snout into the leafy ground. Its nose does not become blocked because the nostrils are narrow slits on each side. A hedgehog's nose is always wet. This seems to make it easier to smell food.

The hedgehog's small, rounded ears can easily hear the sounds of possible danger, and the movements of insects on the ground.

To illustrate the hedgehog's ear clearly, the thick
hair which usually covers it has been removed.

WHERE HEDGEHOGS LIVE

Hedgehogs live in gardens, orchards, and in the countryside. At night, they wander from place to place, searching for food. Hedgehogs have no special territory.

The day nest

During the day the hedgehog sleeps in a nest, hidden under a log, hedge, or other safe place. Because it is a wanderer, the hedgehog needs to build a new nest every few days.

The hedgehog carries leaves and grass in its mouth to the nesting site, and makes a pile about the size of a football. It then turns around and around in the middle of the pile, smoothing out a hollow to sleep in. Before going to sleep, the hedgehog hides itself with a blanket of leaves and grass.

Hedgehog with nesting
material in its mouth.

WHAT HEDGEHOGS EAT

The hedgehog eats spiders, grubs, caterpillars, and many other small garden insects.

On a quiet, still evening, the garden hedgehog may be heard snuffling through leaf litter, rummaging and digging in search of insects.

It munches crunchy insects noisily, and smacks its lips after eating juicy worms. If enjoying a meal from the cat's dinner plate, the hedgehog will make loud slurping sounds. No wonder they are called hedge*hogs*!

Don't give milk to your garden hedgehog. Milk may cause sickness which can kill it. Feed it only raw minced meat or tinned cat food.

Because hedgehogs wander about in dirty places, they can pass on germs to a person who touches them. These germs may cause that person to become ill. You should always wash your hands after touching a hedgehog.

Cats will often share a feeding bowl with a hedgehog.

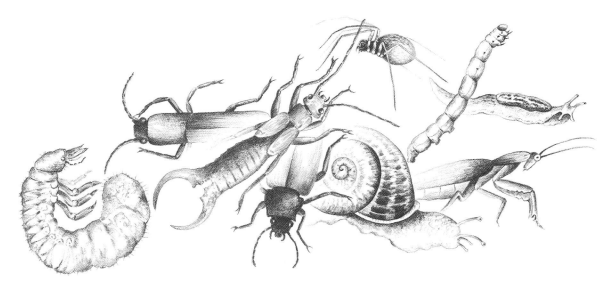

Typical hedgehog food.

How HEDGEHOGS BREED

Breeding occurs in the warm summer months. The two hedgehogs may circle each other for hours. When the female is ready to mate, she smooths her spines very flat so that the male hedgehog can mate with her without being hurt by her prickles.

The female hedgehog remains pregnant for about 40 days. The exact time is not known, as it seems to vary.

The male hedgehog does not help raise the baby hedgehogs. Instead he wanders about all summer, mating with other females and searching for food.

The nursery nest

The nursery nest is built in the same way as the day nest, but is much larger. The nursery nest will need to sleep a mother hedgehog and up to seven babies. It is built two days before the birth of the young hedgehogs.

This female hedgehog has smoothed her spines very flat, to enable the male to mount her prickly back and mate with her.

The baby hedgehog

A baby hedgehog is born without spines. On the skin of its back are two rows of small lumps that are spines under the skin. Within two hours of birth, the spines begin to poke out of the skin. The baby hedgehog soon has a prickly coat of white spines.

As the baby hedgehog grows, it slowly sprouts more and more spines. These are now a brownish colour. In about three weeks the young hedgehog looks like its parents.

By the time a hedgehog is four months old, it has a set of strong teeth for crunching its food.

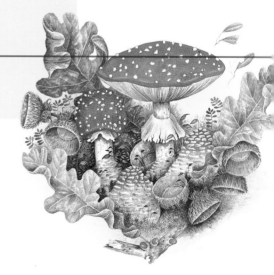

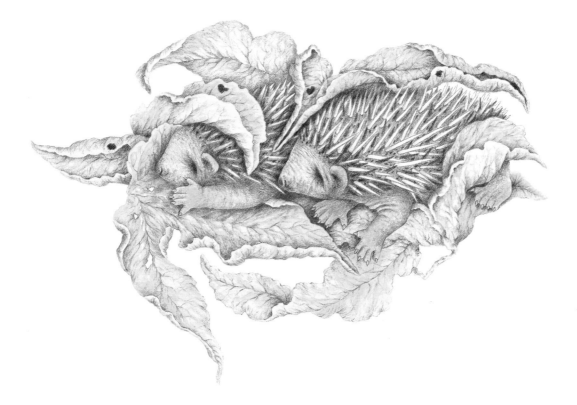

These baby hedgehogs are about five days old,
and are still blind and deaf. In about two weeks
their eyes and ears will open enabling them to
see and hear.

Feeding young hedgehogs

The young hedgehogs drink their mother's milk from two rows of nipples, which are on the outer edges of the mother's soft underside. This means that the prickly babies can feed without crawling underneath their mother's soft belly and hurting her with their sharp spines.

When the young hedgehogs are about three weeks old, they leave the nest at night with their mother. They snuffle about looking for food, but don't eat anything. When they return to the nest to sleep, they drink milk from their mother.

At five weeks of age, the babies are eating solid food, and drinking their mother's milk less often. They go out at night with their mother until they are about eight weeks old. Then they are ready to wander away and live a life on their own.

Dangers to the young

When danger threatens the nursery, the mother hedgehog sometimes shifts her babies to a new nest, but usually the young hedgehogs die a sad death. One sniff at the nest by an animal, or one peep into the nursery by a human, is danger enough to make the mother hedgehog kill her own babies. Sometimes, she may run away and not return to the nest. Her babies may then starve to death, or be killed when they wander from the nursery.

Many young hedgehogs become orphans if the mother runs off when danger threatens, or if she dies, usually by accident.

When the mother doesn't return to the nest, the baby hedgehogs quickly become cold and hungry, and cry loudly. If they are still deaf and blind, they will starve or die from the cold. If they can see and hear, however, they will leave the nest and try to find their mother. They die because they can't feed themselves, or are killed by predators.

These hedgehogs are doomed
as their nest has been disturbed.

Hedgehog HABITS

Nobody knows why hedgehogs have a strange habit of spitting on themselves! Using its tongue, a hedgehog will place large foamy blobs of spit (saliva) on its spines.

This is not to get rid of fleas, because even clean, healthy hedgehogs spit on themselves. Nor is it to attract a mate, as baby hedgehogs also spit on their spines. Studies have shown that it is not done to create an odour, nor to soothe itchy skin, nor to heal a wound. No sensible explanation can be given.

Voice

The hedgehog usually makes snuffling, grunting sounds. But if it is hurt or frightened, it screams and cries loudly. The squeals of a baby hedgehog sound like a bird.

24

These young hedgehogs are investigating the nest entrance.
If they should wander and become lost,
they would cry loudly for their mother.

HIBERNATION

Hedgehogs hibernate because food is very hard to find in the winter. The cold weather kills off most of the insects and grubs that hedgehogs eat.

During hibernation

During hibernation, the hedgehog's heart rate slows until it seems hardly to beat at all, and the hedgehog takes only one breath every few minutes. Its body is very cold to touch and it seems to be dead. The hedgehog does not move or eat during the winter months. It lies hidden from view in a warm, safe hollow covered by leaves and grass.

Before hibernating, the hedgehog eats enough food to make its body very fat. Then, while it is hibernating, the hedgehog's body feeds itself on its white fat, so it does not starve to death. The brown fat in its body is like a cosy blanket which keeps it warm.

This hedgehog's nest is hidden from view. A
hibernating hedgehog lies in a warm, safe hollow
under the log. It can be seen only if the leaves
and grass of the nesting material are removed.

ENEMIES OF THE HEDGEHOG

A ball of prickles

Because hedgehogs have the prickly protection of their spines, they have few enemies.

When alarmed, the hedgehog rolls itself up into a prickly ball. The spines poke out in all directions.

To become a ball, the hedgehog first tucks its head, tail end, and feet underneath its body. To hide these soft parts completely, the hedgehog then pulls tight a special muscle. It is like pulling a draw-string on a bag to close it tightly shut. The hedgehog's head, tail end and feet are now safely hidden away inside the prickly bag.

This young hedgehog has not yet learned how
to roll up. Its soft parts are still exposed to
danger. By the time it is about two weeks old, it
will be able to roll into a tight ball.

Accidents

Millions of hedgehogs are killed by accident each year. They are run over by cars, they are accidentally killed by garden tools and farm machinery, and sometimes they starve to death if trapped in a cattle-stop (grid).

Although hedgehogs are good swimmers, they often drown when trapped in steep-sided garden ponds and swimming pools. They also die after eating poisoned garden grubs. Hibernating hedgehogs are sometimes killed by fire or flood.

People

Many unkind people still kill hedgehogs, believing that they eat birds' eggs and birds, and that they also spread disease.

A hedgehog is not a pest. In fact, it is a great help to most people, as it eats many garden insect pests.

Hedgehogs are good swimmers.

INDEX